# HANNAH
## goes to
# Nursery

by Helen and Clive Dorman

*Paediatric Consultant:*
Dr Huw R Jenkins MA MD FRCP FRCPCH

CP Publishing

When Hannah goes to nursery she meets lots of new friends.

Let us say hello to Hannah, the other girls and boys of Ham Nursery, and their teacher.

Hello Hannah.

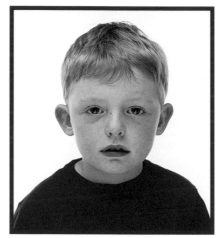

Hello Anthony.

Hello Tilly.

Hello Riwaj.

Hello Felicity – hello 'mouse'!

Hello Bud.

Nursery is a very exciting and busy place. Let us turn the pages and find out what Hannah and her friends are going to do at nursery today.

Hello Lewis.

Hello Tina.
Tina is their teacher.

Hello Lauren.

Hannah is going into the nursery with her teacher Tina.

She is waving goodbye to her mummy.

Sometimes she feels sad when she leaves her mummy.

Hannah is holding Tina's hand, which makes her feel better.

Hannah is sitting on Tina's lap. Hannah feels happy with her thumb in her mouth and holding Tina's hair.

Tina calls the register. She calls out all the children's names, one at a time, to check if they are in class today.

When Tina calls their name, they say:

'Yes Tina'!

After the register it is news time.

During news time the girls and boys can tell everyone about something that is special to them.

Hannah is telling everyone that she has two older brothers.

Do you have a brother or sister?

1 Tina is showing Anthony, Hannah, Tilly and Lewis how to do dot-to-dot drawing.

2 Look at Anthony drawing a straight line!

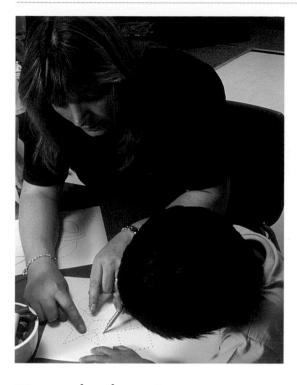

3 Tina helps Lewis to draw round the star.

4 Hannah is being very careful.

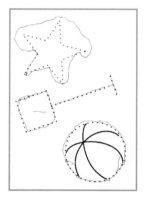

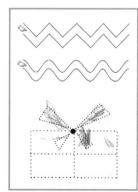

**Anthony**　　　**Hannah**　　　**Tilly**　　　**Lewis**

Here are the pictures drawn by Anthony, Hannah, Tilly and Lewis.

Do you like dot-to-dot drawing and colouring?

1 Hannah, Felicity and Riwaj are looking at themselves in mirrors. Do you know why?

2 Because today they are going to make a face. Felicity is cutting and Tina helps Riwaj to stick.

3 Hannah is sticking.    4 Riwaj thinks it is funny.

5 Here are the faces they have made.

What colour is your hair?

What colour are your eyes?

1 Tilly, Hannah and Anthony have put on aprons because they are going to paint.

2 Anthony tells Hannah all about his painting.

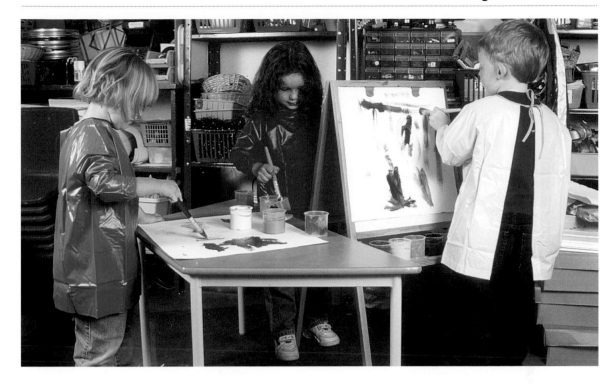

3 Can you see what colour paint Tilly is using?

4 Tilly and Hannah have decided to do some hand painting.

Hannah sometimes likes to get messy when she is painting.

Here are Hannah's, Tilly's and Anthony's paintings. Even though we may not understand what they have painted, they are very special paintings.

Hannah painted **A messy cat**

Tilly painted **Just paint**

Anthony painted **Roads**

Lewis, Tina, Bud, Lauren and Hannah are going to make dough together.

**1** Tina is pouring the flour out of the packet into a bowl.

---

## Easy Dough Recipe

*Makes a good dollop!*
*Takes about 10 minutes*

*You will need*
2 cups of flour
1 cup of salt
1 spoon of oil
1 spoon of cream of tartar
  (optional, as this helps to preserve
  the dough and also keeps it pliable)
1 cup of water
a few drops of food colouring

*What to do*
Put the flour, salt and oil into a large mixing bowl and mix well. Whilst stirring, slowly add one cup of water.

Add a few drops of food colouring to the remaining water. Carefully pour into the mixture, a little at a time, and mix until smooth. It is always good to use your hands.

If the mixture is too wet, sprinkle in some more flour. If it is too dry, add a little more water.

When finished, the dough can be stored in an airtight container, or a plastic food bag.

*Note:* You can make more or less of the dough by adjusting the measurements proportionally.

---

**4** One at a time, Tina pours the oil onto each child's spoon.

**7** The children are stirring the mixture with their spoons.

**2** Bud has just poured his cup of flour into the mixing bowl.

**3** Next, they measure out the cupfuls of salt.

**5** They are stirring the mixture. Hannah is adding the water.

**6** Now Hannah is adding the water with red colouring.

**8** Now they are all mixing the dough with their hands.

**9** Bud and Lauren are modelling the new dough.

Tilly, Anthony and Hannah are dressing up.

Hannah, Anthony and Tilly are busy
playing 'let's pretend'.

Do you like playing 'let's pretend'?
What is your favourite 'let's pretend' game?

Lauren, Bud and Lewis have gone outside with Tina to learn all about plants and seeds, and how they grow.

1 Tina is holding some flowering plants for Lauren to smell.
Tina explains that different plants have different smells.

2 Now it is Bud's turn. He is smelling some herbs.
Herbs are plants we use in cooking.

3 Tina explains that seeds need earth to grow into plants. Lauren, Bud and Lewis are filling the plant pots with earth and they are putting in the seeds.

4 Riwaj comes to help. He is watering the seeds in the pots. The seeds will need to be watered often so that the seeds can grow into plants.

1 It is now playtime. All the children like playing in the sandpit.
Can you point to Riwaj, Lewis, Hannah, Bud, Anthony, Tilly, Lauren and Felicity?
Oops, Felicity! Where is 'mouse'?

2 Lewis is going to fill the buckets with sand!

3 Hannah likes swinging on the tyre.

4 Lauren and Bud are racing on their bikes!

1 Hannah is in the toilet.
When she has finished
she will wash her hands.
Do you know why?

2 The children wash their hands after playtime
because they are going to eat and drink.
Do you know why we wash our hands
before we eat and drink?

3 Today, some of the girls and boys are going to taste lots of different foods.

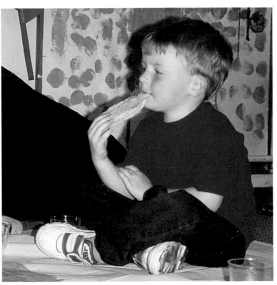

4 Hannah is offering Tilly an olive to try.

5 Anthony is tasting a popadum.

1 Tina asks if anyone would like some carrots. What other food can you see?

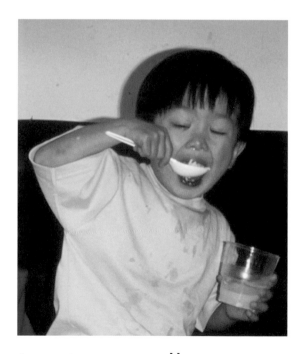

2 Lewis is really enjoying some rice!

3 Bud is drinking up all his orange juice.

1 Anthony, Hannah and Tilly are clapping.
Lewis, Lauren and Bud are playing the music.

3 Now it is tidy up time.
Hannah is putting the
bongos in the crate.

2 Lauren and Bud are
having great fun.

It will soon be home time.

All the children sit down quietly whilst Tina reads a story.

Felicity's 'mouse' joins in too.

Now it is home time. The special things the children have made are given to them to take home. Hannah's messy cat painting is still wet, so it will have to wait until tomorrow to come home!

Hannah's mummy has arrived and Hannah is running to give her mummy a big 'hello' hug and kiss.

She wants to tell mummy all about her busy day at nursery.

Can you name everyone on these pages?
Do you think the girls and boys have had a
busy day at nursery?
What was your favourite activity?

Bye bye ......

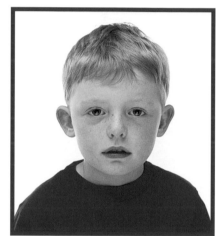

Bye bye ......

Bye bye ......

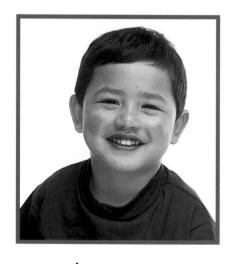

Bye bye ......

Bye bye ......
and bye bye ......

Bye bye ......

Now it is time to say bye bye to
Hannah, Anthony, Tilly, Lewis,
Riwaj, Felicity and 'mouse', Bud, Lauren,
and of course, their teacher, Tina. Bye bye!

Bye bye ......

Bye bye ......

Bye bye ......

## Nursery: you and your child

Starting at nursery is a very big step for you and your child. For many children it will be the first time they have been left with unfamiliar adults and children in a structured environment.

For your child, leaving you and being expected to join in activities may come easily, but many find the whole experience traumatic – crying, clinging to you and refusing to let you go. *'Why can't you stay? Why are you leaving me with all these strangers in a strange place? Will you ever come back to me once you have gone? Will I ever see you again?'*

Emotions can vary: one day happy, the next day not. When you return you may be greeted with tears, even though the teacher assures you there have been no problems during the session. These tears are the same as those shown by adults at an emotional reunion – expressing their love and a huge sense of relief: *'I've missed you and I'm pleased you have come back to me.'*

You may notice changes at home. For example, reverting to a more baby-like past: wanting to be spoon-fed, bed-wetting that is out of character, or generally being less cooperative. These are all perfectly normal emotional reactions. By taking a step back into a more secure past and reliving it, your child feels more able to cope with an uncertain present. Remember, every individual is different and your child's emotions are *very* real. This can be a stressful time for all the family.

Don't worry: with patience, reassurance and understanding your child *will* settle down into the new environment, loving the fun and fulfilment nursery school can offer.

## The importance of nursery education

Nursery education is a vitally important first step on the road to learning. Nursery encourages the development of self expression and social skills which are the fundamental ingredients that go to make a well balanced child, and these are more important than its function of introducing the three R's.

A high self esteem and the ability to master social skills are essential for success in society, and forming friendships is an integral part of our make-up. At nursery, children are encouraged to develop these skills and are brought together to work in group and individual activities. Some can find this difficult. At this early age children have only limited emotional experiences to draw upon and some who may be feeling insecure can express this by biting, pushing, scatching, poking or hitting. This aggressive behaviour can be hard for other children and parents to accept, but patience and understanding should be the first course of action. It is difficult to offer general advice, as each individual reponds differently to the circumstances in which they find themselves. Your nursery teacher will be aware of this and can advise you on how best to deal with the situation.

## About this book

In this book the authors offer an insight into the structure and range of activities to be found at a typical nursery. It is not intended to be a guide to how every nursery is run. This book also attempts to show just how important the five senses – sight, sound, taste, touch and smell – are to a child's development and how they can be incorporated into everyday play.

First published in 2000 by CP Publishing
Richmond, Surrey, United Kingdom

Text Copyright © 1998 Helen & Clive Dorman
Photographs Copyright © 1998 Helen Dorman
This edition Copyright © 2000 The Children's Project Ltd

Helen and Clive Dorman have asserted their moral right to be identified as the authors of this work in accordance with the Copyright, Design and Patents Act 1988.

ISBN 1 903275 02 4

Printed in Hong Kong

## Acknowledgements

We would like to thank Ham Nursery, Richmond for their cooperation. Special thanks to Georgina Llewellyn and Tina Maberley and the children, Anthony, Tilly, Lewis, Riwaj, Felicity, Bud, Lauren and, of course, Hannah, who were all wonderful.